Instagram Influencers

How I make $10,000 a month through Influencer Marketing

Pamela Russell

© Copyright 2014 by Pamela Russell
All rights reserved.

This document is geared towards providing exact and reliable information in regards to the topic and issue covered. The publication is sold with the idea that the publisher is not required to render accounting, officially permitted, or otherwise, qualified services. If advice is necessary, legal or professional, a practiced individual in the profession should be ordered.

Legal Notice: From a Declaration of Principles which was accepted and approved equally by a Committee of the American Bar Association and a Committee of Publishers and Associations. In no way is it legal to reproduce, duplicate, or transmit any part of this document in either electronic means or in printed format. Recording of this publication is strictly prohibited and any storage of this document is not allowed unless with written permission from the publisher. All rights reserved.

Disclaimer Notice: The information provided herein is stated to be truthful and consistent, in that any liability, in terms of inattention or otherwise, by any usage or abuse of any policies, processes, or directions contained within is the solitary and utter responsibility of the recipient reader. Under no circumstances will any legal responsibility or blame be held against the publisher for any reparation, damages, or monetary loss due to the information herein, either directly or indirectly. Respective authors own all copyrights not held by the publisher. The information herein is offered for informational purposes solely, and is universal as so. The presentation of the information is without contract or any type of guarantee assurance.

The trademarks that are used are without any consent, and the publication of the trademark is without permission or backing by the trademark owner. All trademarks and brands within this book are for clarifying purposes only and are the owned by the owners themselves, not affiliated with this document.

Table of contents

Chapter 1 – Getting started 1

Chapter 2 – About the Series 6

Chapter 3 – Understanding the Market 8

Chapter 4 – Publishing Sponsored Posts 12

Chapter 5 - How Much money can you expect? 14

Author's Note - Reaching 1 Million Followers 25

Chapter 6 - How to Find Sponsors 26

Chapter 7 – Affiliate Marketing 32

Chapter 8 - Sell Your Own Product or Service 38

Chapter 9 – Sell Your Own Photos 42

Chapter 10 – Become Active on Multiple Social Media 47

Chapter 11 – The Importance of Photography 49

Conclusion 51

Chapter 1 – Getting started

We have all heard stories of teenagers earning outrageous salaries for posting photos on Instagram. If you haven't here's your first: Essena O'Neill is an 18 year old Australian girl with 500,000 (or 500K) Instagram followers. Brands pay her around $2,000 to upload a single photo wearing their items of clothing.

Inevitably we have all wondered the same question "Could I do it too?". The idea of earning thousands of dollars for simply taking photos, posting them online and sharing a passion with people who admire you is – in some way or another – appealing to everyone.

Unfortunately, we all look up to Instagram channels boasting hundreds of thousands of followers earning thousands of dollars and feel overwhelmed. Their success and their reach is so widespread across all forms of social media it is nearly impossible not be affected.

Their celebrity-like status is admirable, but to many it can also be intimidating. To many it represents a reason to quit before even trying as they think: "I could never reach millions of follower" or "There are so many famous people on Instagram, what can I do?"

Through my decades of experience in large-scale advertising campaigns and years of involvement in social media marketing, I am here to tell you not to worry. An audience of millions can not be built in a day and unfortunately the social media industry is becoming increasingly competitive. You must be patient and work hard to grow your account day after day.

Unfortunately this book will not teach you how to grow an Instagram account. I designed this guide to teach readers how they can start earning money from the Instagram account they already possess. Everyday I see far too many profiles that could easily draw in thousands of dollars per month, but due to a lack of experience and information. With this book I want to change that.

The Social Media marketing industry is booming right now, there are endless opportunities for anyone ready to take them! If you follow the teachings of this book and apply the lessons it presents, you can earn money whether you have 1,000 Instagram followers or 500K.

How Do You make Money on Instagram?

There are many revenue generation streams on Instagram. Personally, I have found the most success with the strategies below:

- **Create Sponsored Content** (see chapters 3-5) – Brands will pay you to advertise and promote their products using your Instagram account, this is how most famous Instagrammer make money. I will show you how to find brands willing to sponsor you, the different types of sponsorships available and how much money you can make.
- **Afilliate Marketing** (see chapter 6) – you promote a product or service to your followers and you receive a commission on their purchase (usually 10-20%). I will show you exactly how to acquire your own affiliate links with major online marketplaces and how to approach brands for unique partnerships.

- **Sell Your Own Product or Service** (see chapter 7) - this is a great way to capitalize on your followers' commitment towards your page. I will show you exactly how to get started on your tshirt business: where you can hire designers, find overseas manufacturers, print t-shirts on-demand and how to set up your own online store.
- **Selling Your Own Photos or Designs** (see chapter 8) – If your Instagram account features a unique brand of photography or digital design, you can build a significant revenue selling digital prints. Personally, I do not follow this route because I am not an expert photographer or graphic designer, but I know of many Instagrammers who use this technique to make thousands of dollars every month. I will show you how to ensure people do not steal your photos or designs and where to effectively sell them online.

I have come across and even experimented with many additional techniques to monetize an Instagram account. Many of these proved far too complex or not successful and for this reason I have chosen not to include them in the above list.

An example of an alternative revenue stream is to collect the emails of your followers and sell it to advertising companies. You can do this by building a simple landing page using Wix.com (it is free!) where visitors can provide an email in exchange of a free gift. I have found this method time-intesive and difficult to scale to a point where you can produce a significant; I no longer use this method on my personal instagram accounts.

Of course, you are free to explore other revenue-generation streams, but in this guide I will only discuss the methods mentioned above. They represent the bread and butter of instagram money generation and can make you tens of thousands of dollars provided you have a large, engaged audience.

How Many Followers Do I Need to make money?

I have been directly involved in the growth and management of Instagram accounts spanning across most subjects you can think of. Regardless, the question I get asked most often does not change: "how many followers do I need to make money on Instagram?"

My answer is: "not as many as you think". Even if your account only has 2,000 followers you can start generating an income today using the techniques described in this book. In fact, it is critical you start monetizing your instagram account as soon as possible.

If your account is small, you will not generate a lot of money at first. However, you will build strong foundations that can support large income streams once your account does grow.

It takes time to learn how the influencer marketing industry works: finding sponsors, negotiating deals and setting up contracts can be complicated. Learning how to make effective use of the most popular online platforms and marketplaces for influencers can be difficult and time-consuming. It is better that you make mistakes when your account is still small: they will cost you less money and have a lower impact on your reputation.

The importance of Engagement for Money Generation

Follower engagement is the most important metric on your page after the total number of followers. Engagement defines how dedicated, committed and loyal your followers are; this is directly proportional to the income you will generate.

There are many different approaches to quantifying user engagement; I like to use the formula below. It provides a good, simple and reliable figure for the engagement of any instagram page.

Engagement = [Average number of likes in last 10 posts] / [Total number of followers]

When you are trying to advertise yourself as a valuable influencer to brands, you must demonstrate a good analytical understanding for your account metrics. Providing a mathematically calculated percentage for your user engagement can make a good impression.

The above metric also helps identify the most valueable influencers. For instance, an influencer with 100K followers and 1% engagement is less valuable to a brand than an influencer with 50K followers but 5% engagement. The latter will drive more traffic and awareness to a brand and therefore should request a higher pay (in spite having less followers).

Chapter 2 – About the Series

My marketing agency develops powerful campaigns that increase a brand's exposure and reputation within a selected market space. The majority of my recent clients are now seeking campaigns built around social media marketing. Of course, a strong Instagram presence would represent the backbone of said strategy.

As a result, I have dedicated a lot of time and energy towards understanding the psychology of the Instagram user: what makes him follow a new page, what affects his engagement and establishing brand loyalty - ultimately maximizing your cash flow and income.

Having worked with a wide variety of pages for a long time now, I have had many opportunities to experiment which techniques lead to Instagram success and which, unfortunately, do not. From these first-hand experiences I have created the Amazon Best-Seller series "Dominating the Instagram Game".

This series was developed for the beginner/amateur Instagram user looking for professional guidance into the ever-changing world of social media. In particular, we will focus on the topics of social media marketing, digital advertisement and generating a monetary income.

However, my explanations can only go *so far*. Please understand this series will challenge and push your understanding of Instagram – we will cover many topics involving digital marketing, photography and PR. To follow along and make the most of these books I need you to be

committed and **passionate** about the material we will cover. Most importantly, you must take the initiative and experiment these techniques in your own social media accounts.

I have been working very hard on structuring the content of this series, but for now only the first publications have been officially released to the public – please stay tuned for the latest releases (my Amazon author page: **www.bit.ly/PamelaRussell**). In the meantime, I would highly appreciate any feedback on the current publications and suggestions for future topics – please leave these in Amazon's official review section.

Are you ready? Ok good - Let's explore how you can generate an income from Instagram!

Chapter 3 – Understanding the Market

"Consumers trust Congress more than brand advertising"

I have been involved in the advertising industry for many decades now and one thing has never changed: **people do not trust ads**.

Whether watching tv, reading a magazine or at the stadium cheering, people demonstrate an inherent lack of trust towards advertisement; unfortunately digital marketing is no different. When browsing the internet, we are now bombarded with pop-up ads, cookie reminders, auto-play video ads and content-blocking ads.

These increasingly intrusive and controlling forms of advertisement have developed an internet browsing experience where users feel monitored, watched and simply unsafe. **There is no more trust.**

Social Media is the exception to the rule. Social media are not sales platforms, they are conversation platforms. They are online destinations where users open up and share their passions, feelings and emotions with their closest friends.

On these websites people are in search for individuals who look, talk and act like them who can deliver engaging and valuable content.

Many of these have acquired a true celebrity status amongst their peers and earn absurd salaries. Many have audiences composed by millions of loyal users who watch every new video or photo as soon as it is posted – these individuals are known as **Influencers**.

The term "Influencer" gets thrown around a lot these days, although everyone has a different definition for it, here's mine:

"An Influencer is an individual who has established a respected online reputation in a particular business, activity or field. Their regular, loyal audience views these individuals as independent, creative trendsetters whose knowledge in a given space is to be trusted and respected"

The ability of today's influencers to persuade millions of people into their own way of thinking is absolutely stunning. Many brands have recognized this opportunity and now hire influencers to give their products reach, authenticity and a real-world presence that could not be achieved with any other form of advertising.

Why do influencers have such a strong ability to *influence* people?

I, and many other marketing experts, have devoted significant time and resources towards explaining this phenomenon. Diving into the entire analysis of the buyer's psychology is well beyond the scope of this books, so here is the short answer:

1. Audience Reach
2. Audience Trust

Reach is easy to buy, but Audience Trust can not be bought: you have to build it.

You can pay a few thousand dollars right now and take control of a billboard that will cross the eyes of ten thousand people, but will they follow its message? Will they trust you?

Brands want to purchase the trust your followers have in you and they are ready to cover you in gold for it. They want to purchase the power you have to influence people's decisions. They want you to convince people *this* product is better than *that* product.

Remember: audience trust is your **only** and most valuable asset, no matter what people tell you. Always cherish it, never compromise it and learn to appreciate its true value.

What is Influencer Marketing?

This new form of advertisement is called *Influencer Marketing* and is truly powerful. I have personally seen a million-dollar company built on the reccomendations of a single influencer: just how powerful is it?

Here are some facts to help you understand this marketing opportunity we are all facing right now within the social media space:
- Instagram has 700 million monthly active users
- social media accounts for over 50% of total time spent online
- 75% of customers seek pre-purchase information on social media
- 90% of customer will make purchasing decisions base on influencer reccomendations
- 84% of customers will make purchasing decisions based on influencer opinions

INFLUENCER MARKETING

Chapter 4 – Publishing Sponsored Posts

We have established why brands intend to work with influencers: they want to leverage the trust your audience has in your opinion to sell their products or services. The most popular technique to achieve this is through sponsored posts.

For people who are new to the business of Instagram sponsorships, it can be very easy to make mistakes and destroy their reputation. As an influencer, you must find a balance between sponsored content to increase revenue and maintaining your integrity as an honest, unbiased content creator who has the best interest of their followers above all else.

Your audience trusts you as an influencer because you only recommend what is, in your opinion, the best product on the market. They trust you because you present yourself as a peer. They trust you because you are recommending a product, not advertising.

If your audience believes you are only pushing products only to make a profit, you will become a 'sell-out'. You are no longer a peer-to-peer relatable figure who is making helpful **suggestions**, you become a salesperson who is trying to make money. Your opinion is no longer trusted and your reputation may never recover.

As an influencer, you are only valuable because of the **trust** followers have towards you. Compromise this trust and your income streams will disappear.

How can you ensure Sponsorships do not compromise your reputation?

There is a simple answer: be **SELECTIVE**. As a rule of thumb you should only promote products that (1)match the best interests of your audience and (2)products you would purchase yourself/genuinely believe in.

Greed is your worst enemy. If you have a small amount of followers, Instagram should not represent your only source of income. You must have freedom to select only the brands that meet your ideals, visions and standards. You must have the freedom to turn down money from products you do not believe in and therefore can not recommend to your audience.

As soon as your audience loses trust in your opinion, your account becomes worthless. Never forget that.

Once you become active in the industry you will see how large brands treat their brand image and reputation above everything else. As a result they are very selective about their influencers. In the same way that you should not promote products you do not believe in, brands do not want to be represented by users they do not believe in. If you already have experience as an Instagram influencer you will know exactly what I am talking about. If you are new to the industry, you will learn very quickly.

Chapter 5- How Much money can you expect?

Most of you will be wondering where to find brands that are willing to pay you in exchange for exposure and product advertising. Do not worry it is not as difficult as most think; in fact it is quite easy! In the next chapter I will cover a number of strategies you can use to find paid sponsorship opportunities today regardless of how many followers you have.

In this chapter I want to clarify what is, in my opinion, a significantly more important issue: **money expectations**. Most of us have heard stories of people making tens of thousands of dollars from Instagram alone and believe it is not an easy, straightforward process. I do it and personally I do enjoy it, but please understand that it is **POSSIBLE, NOT EASY**.

The two most significant parameters that determine your earning potential on Instagram are (1) number of followers and (2) total engagement. Unfortunately these parameters are not the be-all end-all of Instagram cash flow, it is much more complicated than that. There are innumerable factors that come into play such as the market relevance of your page and your chosen revenue generation streams. For this reason, it is very difficult to predict exactly how much money you can generate through sponsorships without a detailed assessment of your profile.

However, I have worked with hundreds of Instagram clients and have acquired a good understanding for the current Instagram sponsorship market. Below I have compiled a list of TYPICAL figures you can expect from different sponsorship strategies based on the number of total followers. I will be discussing the four most common types of Instagram sponsorships found in today's market. Note that if you are a unique influencer such as a well-recognized leader in your market space or you specialize in a very niche sector, your earning figures can vary quite drastically.

The figures presented in the following assume the following conditions:

- medium-good user engagement (2-5% engagement)
- Account based on a well-funded high-demand niche (such as fashion, fitness, nutrition, …)
- Below 1 Million followers (above this figure sponsorship fees can vary immensely)
- Non-repeat, one-off deals (long-term contracts and brand ambassador work can deliver significantly higher earnings)

Caption Sponsorship

You post an image to your Instagram account and in the description you include the link to a brand or another Instagram account, recommending your followers go check it out. Most of these agreements work on a fixed rate, but I have seen variations where a bonus is given if the picture receives a set number of likes/comments.

This is the simplest and least-intrusive type of sponsorship generally practiced in the industry. It generates the smallest income amongst all sponsorship strategies, but allows you to retain full control over the image posted.

Rough Earning Potential

- 50k Followers: $10
- 150K Followers: $15
- 250K Followers: $30
- 750K Followers: $100

What does it look like?

Below is an example of an obviously sponsored caption I found online. You can see that an external Instagram account is presented and followers are funnelled to it. Nevertheless, this sponsorship is not too intrusive: the page owner maintained full control of the image. Those with no experience in Instagram sponsorships might even think the page owner was simply sharing a helpful suggestion with his followers instead of being paid!

Sponsored Image

The process is relatively straightforward: your sponsor sends you a photo, you post it to your Instagram and caption something similar to "courtesy of my good friend: _____" or "great work by: _____". You then provide directions to reach their webpage, online store or Instagram page in the caption and suggest your Instagram followers go and visit.

The main downside of this strategy is that you lose control over the posted image. It can be very difficult to find an image both you and your sponsor agree on: your goal is to maintain "page values" and not come off as a "sell-out", whereas your sponsor wants to push his brand and product as much as possible using logos, brands, offers and links. Remember, your page is only valuable as long as you retain your audience **trust,** so be very selective on what you post**!**

I typically suggest my clients do these types of sponsorships on a time-limited basis, i.e. you agree to remove the picture after a day.

Rough Earning Potential

- 50k Followers: $50/day
- 150K Followers: $150/day
- 250K Followers: $300/day
- 750K Followers: $800/day

What does it look like?

Below I have reported an example of a sponsored image I found online; immediately you can see the image was created by a different account. The original account is tagged in the description to funnel new visitors into visiting the page. You can also see a clear element of **branding** on this image, identifying the creator and sponsor of this image (most sponsored images will contain very obvious element of branding/product placement)

Sponsored Screener

A sponsored screener is when you post the direct screenshot of a website or another Instagram account on your profile, in the attempt of getting YOUR followers interested. This method shows your followers what they will find in the advertised webpage/Instagram account without having to change webpage; this type of advertisement is extremely effective. For this reason, through sponsored screeners you can earn a lot more money than any other sponsorship strategy.

The big earnings, as always, bring also meaningful pitfalls. Posting a screener is a very obvious form of advertisement and it is immediately recognised by all of your active followers. More often than not this form of advertisement will earn you a well-deserved "sell-out" status.

Personally, I do not recommend my Instagram clients pursue this strategy because it can severely damage your reputation and follower trust. However, this is an effecting strategy to raise cash quickly. I do not recommend it, but I want to cover the most relevant sponsorship strategies and discuss their positives (short-term earnings increase) and negatives (risk of ruining audience trust).

Ultimately, it is up to you to decide how to grow and develop your Instagram account and how much sponsored content you are willing to put out in order to earn money. Make sure you do further research into this method and reach out to people who have been along this route to gain first-hand experience. Again, I do not think the short-term cash offers are worth the long-term damages to your reputation.

Should you decide to go down this line, please make sure your sponsorship agreement is on a time-limited basis. Typically, I see that posting screeners for 1-3 hours works best.

Rough Earning Potential

- 50k Followers: $120/3hours
- 150K Followers: $300/3hours
- 250K Followers: $600/3hours
- 750K Followers: $1,400/3hours

What does it look like?

I found an example of a screener ad from the same account as before (this particular user pursues A LOT of sponsorship). You can immediately tell this post is an obvious, blatant advertisement. At the same time you can also see how effective this method is in advertising another Instagram page or website to your followers. Again, notice the link and funnelling in the post caption.

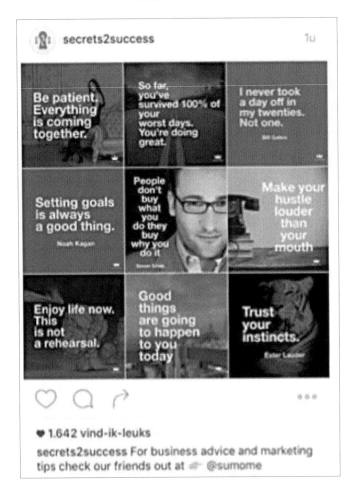

Sponsored link in Bio

Currently Instagram allows for only one clickable URL on your profile. This can only be posted on your profile BIO and nowhere else. Clearly this link is very visible on your profile and it will be receiving a lot of attention from your followers. This link is one of the most valuable assets at your disposal to earn cash.

Personally, I find that placing an affiliate link on this location generates the best results (see chapter 6 to learn more about affiliate marketing). However, there are brands offering very good offers for sponsored BIO link placement. If you come across an offer that you find appealing, I suggest taking it on short time-intervals (1-3 hours) and leaving your primary affiliate link the rest of the time.

Pro Tip: you can redirect your follower's attention towards the URL by writing "link in the description" in your captions.

Working with my clients I find that sponsored/affiliate links in the BIO do not create a perception of "selling out" amongst your followers, instead they represent a great income generation stream. I recommend this strategy to all my clients!

Pro Tip: if your link is long, bulky or contains strange words use a link shortener (see chapter 6)

Rough Earning Potential

- 50k Followers: $60/3hours
- 150K Followers: $120/3hours
- 250K Followers: $250/3hours
- 750K Followers: $700/3hours

What does it look like?

Below you can see the Instagram BIO of a popular fitness account. In the BIO he provides the link to a sales page, where his followers can purchase training programs and a variety of fitness-related products. This particular Instagrammer uses this URL location to drive traffic and increase sales, generating a very large income. You too can make a lucrative use of this opportunity by adding affiliate/sponsored links in your BIO.

Author's Note- Reaching 1 Million Followers

As I previously mentioned, the primary purpose of this book is to show readers how to start earning money from their **current** Instagram account. Unfortunately, for many of you the generated income will fail to meet your original expectations.

There is only one definite way to significantly increase your Instagram income in the long-term: **GROW YOUR AUDIENCE**!

In one of my previous book instalments I presented a detailed blueprint guide designed to grow any Instagram account to 1 million followers in 6 months. Yes, it is an ambitious goal but by no means impossible.

I have received a lot of positive responses on this book and I highly recommend you check it out. It has helped many people grow their Instagram audience and drastically increase their income as a result.

Chapter 6- How to Find Sponsors

I have already stressed the importance of being selective when promoting a brand. But many Instagram newcomers are interested in a much more fundamental issue: **Where do I find sponsors**?

When you run a large Instagram account, brand PRs will approach you directly asking for sponsorship. My Instagram page has 1.2 Million followers at 4% engagement and on average I receive 2-5 sponsorship offers every day.

For smaller isntagram accounts it can be more difficult to find brands willing to sponsor you. Certainly, for those who have never worked with brands on Instagram, finding sponsors must seem impossible.

FEAR NOT: finding brands willing to sponsor you is much easier than you think. There are two main strategies for influencers to connect with a brand: (1)Use online marketplaces that connect influencers and brands sharing similar values and (2)Contact brands that interest you directly

Use Online Influencer Marketplaces

Online marketplaces have been created to put influencers and brands in direct contact. These marketplaces are the perfect opportunity for small influencers to place their profiles under the eyes of brands seeking exposure on instagram. If you have no previous experience in paid instagram sponsorships, I recommend you only find sponsors through these marketplaces at least for a few months.

These marketplaces are an excellent learning tool for anyone who is new to the Influencer Marketing. Here you gain fast exposure to many different brands, types of sponsorships, negotiation strategies and see how competing influencers market themselves to brands.

If, for the first time in your career, you contact brands directly and negotiate a sponsorship agreement without knowing the industry, you will most likely get ripped off.

Below I have reported my favourite influencer marketplaces, here you will find thousands of brands offering pay in exchange for brand sponsorship. You will also be able to browse the profiles of competitor influencers. I recommend you look into all of these platforms and become active in one or two of the ones you like the most.

My personal favourites:

Shoutcart.com – this platform allows influencers to sell shoutouts directly to brands. All influencers advertise their price, relevant field and profile information: such as number of followers, isntagram link, etc. This platform is targeted towards single use instagram advertising, not long-term brand collaborations.I highly recommend you use this as a first experience into the world of paid instagram advertising. By viewing the profiles and prices of all influencers in your industry, you can develop a good understanding for the market prices and what you can ask.

Here is a screens of how brands search for influencers using this platform:

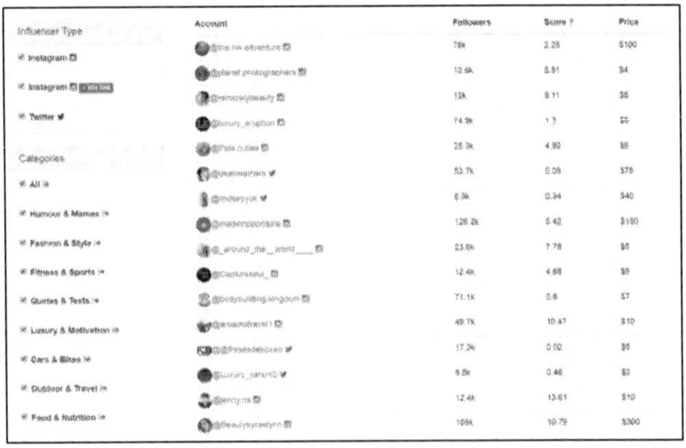

Grapevinelogic.com – Grapevine is a marketplace that aims to develop large-scale long-term marketing relationship between influencers and brands; they only work with Instagram and Youtube. You can find massive brands on here, such as L'Oreal and LG which regularly recruit and pay influencers using this platform. To register you need at least 5,000 followers on Instagram or 10,000 subscribers on YouTube. Afterwards, you can personally view the proposals of different brands, pitch them on what you can offer and negotiate the terms of your work. You can assess the success of your content using bespoke analytics and you will get paid directly and securely through this platform.

Other excellent resources to find paid sponsorship as an Influencer:

FohrCard.com – This platform can appear a bit more complex. Here you can list all your social media profiles and blogs to build an overall profile or "card" that showcases all your influencing abilities. You can view a list of brands and their requirements, select the brands that match your desire and pitch them for an opportunity to work together.

IndaHash.com – You need at least 700 Instagram followers to sign up on this platform. Brands advertise their marketing campaigns on this website and influencers can choose to participate and get paid by posting content on Instagram with the specified hashtags.

Approaching Brands Yourself

I have clients who find themselves with a flourishing Instagram account, earning thousands of dollars per month and receiving new sponsorship proposals every day. At one point or another, most of these clients approach me asking the same question: "**I love this brand, can I get sponsored by them?**"

This can be a very tricky question and sometimes the answer my answer has to be "**you can't**". It is important to understand that not all brands are active on Instagram and not all brands are available to sponsor new influencers. Further yet, some brands only sponsor superstars. For instance, even if you have 300K followers on Instagram you simply cannot be sponsored from Chanel or Nike, who focus their sponsorships on international supermodels and elite athletes.

If you wish to receive sponsorship from a particular brand, you should verify that this brand is **already** sponsoring Instagram accounts similar to you. If they are not, I suggest passing on this brand unless you are willing to deal with an endless stream of PR and sales people who are probably completely unaware of social media marketing and will ultimately reject your proposals.

If the brand of interest is already sponsoring Instagrammers like you, then great! Now you must attract the brand's attention on social media and show them how you can provide **Value** to their brand.

If you wish to pursue sponsorship with a particular brand I recommend having at least 50,000 followers. It is very time consuming to pursue a single brand and often may prove an unsuccessful pursuit. You must have clear value to offer and a large, dedicated following.

If you are determined to go down this path, these are the most effective strategies you can employ:

Hasthag the brand

Hashtags are a very simple and effective way to attract a brand's attention on Instagram. Find out what hashtags your particular brand responds to and add it to your posts. The brand's digital marketing section will see your posts and your content. Most brands have small social media departments and with the right hashtags, you can draw significant attention to your page.

If your page is of outstanding quality and absolutely stuns the brand's PR department, you might even receive an offer for sponsorship, although I have rarely seen this happen. In this strategy, your main goal is to attract the brand's attention. You are trying to establish the foundations for a future sponsorship deal.

Contact other sponsored pages

Search for other Instagram pages that are sponsored by this brand and contact them. Send them a DM on Instagram and start a conversation. Discuss your Instagram experiences and the passions for the fields you have in common. If you feel like they are approachable and friendly, ask about their brand sponsorship and how they got it. Express your interest in a potential opportunity and ask for suggestions on how to receive a similar sponsorship. They might provide useful guidance in terms of who to contact or any particular features they look for in their influencers.

Contact directly & sell yourself

Finally, this is the be-all end-all step. You have gathered information, you have attracted their attention and you are sure your Instagram account fits all requirements for sponsorship by this brand. Now it is time to make your sale pitch and convince them you can be a valuable asset to this brand.

Many brands have a "brand ambassador programme" advertised on their website where you can apply; if your brand does, then I suggest contacting them through that portal. If they do not, then contact them directly on their Instagram page. When contacting them take the following approach:

- Briefly explain who you are and what your page is about
- Express why you are genuinely interested in the brand
- Explain why your page values meets the brand's vision
- Seek information into their sponsorship program/opportunities
- Explain how you can bring value and exposure to their brand through social media

Chapter 7 – Affiliate Marketing

Affiliate marketing is one of the most popular and effective strategies to monetize any online audience that looks up to you. The underlying idea is simple: you promote a product or service to your followers and you receive a commission on their purchase.

The arrangement is generally very straightforward: the brand provides you with a unique, trackable link to a landing page where your followers can make the purchase. Although I have seen many variations in affiliate sponsorships, for instance some brands also offer a commission for every time the link is clicked.

Unfortunately, links are not allowed anywhere on Instagram except for your BIO. This means you cannot add affiliate links in your posts, and can only have one active affiliate link at any one time. On other platforms such as YouTube, where you can add an unlimited amount of links in your video description, you come across users who provide tens of affiliate links with every new video they release.

Placing a sponsored link in the IO is a popular and lucrative alternative to an affiliate link, brands will pay good fees for that prime advertising location. Visit chapter 4 to learn more about brand sponsorship and sponsored links in your bio.

Promo codes are a popular alternative to affiliate links, because you can add them to the caption of every Instagram post you release. These are unique trackable codes the brand associates exclusively with your audience. When used, these links will typically provide customers with special discounts or offers and you will receive a commission on their purchase. The main question Instagrammers newcomers find themselves asking is:

How can I arrange affiliate memberships with brands?

There are two main approaches to affiliate marketing on Instagram: (1) affiliation with major online retailers and (2) exclusive affiliate partnerships with online brands

Affiliate Programs with Major Online Retailers

Many affiliate programs are so mind-numbingly simple to arrange, I make all my social media clients to do it even if they only have 500 followers! Major online retailers provide very simple, fully automated online platforms which are quick and straightforward to set up, my favourite is the Amazon Affiliate Program.

Affiliate-program.amazon.com – Go to this URL and create an account. You can search any product on Amazon and you will receive a custom link to this product that is exclusively identified with your affiliate account. Whenever a person using this link purchases the advertised product, you will receive a 10% commission on their **total** Amazon purchase paid directly to your bank account. Even if they do not buy the product you advertised, but go on to purchase different products you still receive a 10% commission on anything they purchase (if they arrived on Amazon through your link). This particular feature can lead to incredible pay, especially under Christmas time.

Pro Tip: you can create an affiliate link for yourself every time you need to shop on Amazon to receive a 10% 'refund' on anything you purchase yourself!

There are many other online platforms that provide similar affiliate programs and they typically offer 20% commissions. I recommend you check them out, although Amazon remains my favourite because it is a very well-known reputable site where your audience will feel secure – remember the importance of establishing and maintain audience trust.

Clickbank.com – This is a very well-known online destination for affiliate programs. This marketplace primarily deals with online courses and offers a 20% commission. Items on this website typically fall in the 50-200$ range, which leads to nice and beefy commissions! I highly recommend checking out the products they offer and see if you find anything that would appeal to your followers.

RewardStyle.com – You cannot simply join this platform, but can only be invited into it. This is a premium online destination for fashion influencers only, where you will find clothing and accessories to advertise for a 20% commission.

Exclusive Affiliate Partnerships with Online Brands

Setting up an affiliate relationship with major online retailers is a straightforward, automated process that takes almost no time at all, working with brands directly is very different. Becoming affiliated to small & medium brands is not altogether different from receiving sponsorship: you must contact them directly explaining why you can be a valuable asset to their social media presence. They will evaluate your profile and eventually they may decide to take you on as part of their team of social media influencers.

The only difference between sponsorship and affiliation is that, instead of asking for money directly, you are asking for a promo code or link that will generate you money. The process for obtaining sponsorship is described in detail in chapter 5, you can use the same approach to seek brand affiliation, here is an overview:

- Briefly explain who you are and what your page is about
- Express why you are genuinely interested in the brand
- Explain why your page values meets the brand's vision
- Seek information into their affiliate program/opportunities
- Explain how you can bring value and exposure to their brand through social media

Use bit.ly

Many affiliate links can be very long and bulky, you run the risk of clogging up your bio with a link that is 3-lines full of alphanumeric symbols. I recommend using link shorteners such as **bit.ly**. This one is free to use - you can sign up easily at www.bit.ly

I really like this tool because (1) it minimizes the size of any URL link to a few characters and (2) you can track how many times the link has been clicked over time and from which countries.

Take a look at the link presented below; this is the URL I have taken directly from my Amazon Author page: it is long, bulky and difficult to copy. If you are posting a similar link in your Instagram bio it will appear messy, difficult to spot and will consume a lot of space (remember your Instagram bio is limited to 300 characters!). Now, take a look at the reduced link. When clicked it still redirects users to the same web page, but it is short, compact and easy to follow!

Example of a long link:

https://www.amazon.com/Pamela-Russell/e/B0718YP6RB/ref=dp_byline_cont_book_1

Example of reduced link:

http://amzn.to/2runkwy

Bit.ly also offers the opportunity to track how many times your URLs have been clicked over time as well as the origin of these clicks. Below I have shown the information bit.ly provides for one of my links, which has been clicked 213 times.

Chapter 8- Sell Your Own Product or Service

By now, you must think the only way to make money from Instagram is to "sell out" and promote all types of products developed by other brands. Well, here's another option: CREATE YOUR OWN PRODUCTS.

Creating your own products can be an excellent way to take your Instagram account to next level: it can help increase reach and user engagement while building you a profit. As an influencer, your knowledge in a particular marketplace should help you understand what products your audience is interested in, what they would like to purchase and at what price point.

Remember: when creating Instagram products emphasize you have the best interests of your audience in mind. Tell them you created the product because you could find nothing like it in the market, explain to them why it's unique and ABSOLUTELY show them the behind-the-scenes process of creating the product, from its initial design to its pre-launch briefing.

If you are going to sell products or services online you will need an online shop where your audience can make the purchase. My recommended options is Shopify.com - the single best online resource for small and medium businesses to set up an online store.

Shopify.com – Shopify is a complete online ecommerce platform that allows you to create a professional and completely personalized website without requiring any knowledge of web programming, such as CSS or HTML. Shopify is better than WordPress for online shops, because it was built for ecommerce only and offers a whole variety of templates and features that will make online sales as straightforward as possible. You can link your followers to your online store where they can purchase your products directly from you.

Setting up your personal online store and the creation of your own products will require significant initial investments, both in terms of time and money. However, once set up you will have established a long-term semi-passive income strategy that requires little work to maintain. Your followers will be happy to take part in your new initiatives and support you in the purchase of merchandise.

If your products sell well, you can choose to develop a real, independent brand that you can market to everyone, even beyond your followers. You may even wish to hire other influencers to push your products using some of the sponsorship strategies mentioned in chapters 3-5.

What products should you create?

I have come into contact with a vast number of influencers spanning across all types of businesses and fields. To those who wish to create their own products, I always recommend starting with t-shirts with their logo/iconic images on it. Your 'brand' or your appeals to your followers and you will find that many of them are eager to support your social media journey by purchasing merchandise. In order to justify the up-front investments required to successfully design, manufacture, advertise and ship your own t-shirts, I usually recommend having at least 10,000 well-engaged Instagram followers

Please, make sure that making money is not your primary aim in this endeavour (or at least don't make your followers think it is). If your products are overpriced to make high margins, people will start calling you a "sell-out" and you will lose followers. If your price is high due to a low production volume, make sure you say it!

Although you might not make money from your first batch of t-shirts, the process will teach you a lot about the work required to create a real product and manage a real business. You will have to work with designers to produce logos and t-shirt patterns. You will have to find manufacturers and collaborate with them to create a product that meets your quality requirements – believe me it is never easy. You will have to deal with shipping, inventory, quality complaints and manage returns.

Successfully creating and launching a product to market is very different to running an Instagram page; it requires very different skills. By starting with a low risk product such as t-shirts, you will acquire a broad understanding for the go-to-market process and, in case of small accidents or failures, the consequences will be limited. Nevertheless, you will gain invaluable experience which will prepare you for the creation and production of any future high-investment product you are planning to create.

Useful Resources to get you started

Fiverr.com – on this website you can hire graphic designers who work for very cheap. Great to obtain logo or design samples for your first t-shirts.

On-demand Printing – this means t-shirts are printed as soon as you receive an order. This method means you have no inventory, no initial-investment and risks are minimized. I HIGHLY recommend this approach for smaller volume strategies.

These are my favourite on-demand Shopify apps that take care of on-demand t-shirt printing. Check them out!
- apps.shopify.com/print-aura
- apps.shopify.com/printful

Alibaba.com – this is an online platform that connects you with overseas large-scale manufacturers. Working with this website can be quite tricky, you must learn to deal with import/export taxes, specialized manufacturing processes and work with long lead times (i.e. it takes a long time for you to receive a test sample from Malaysia and verify its quality!) I suggest this website if you are considering ordering over 100 t-shirts.

designious.com/t-shirt-designs – this is a great marketplace where you can browse thousands of t-shirt designs and, if you encounter any that you absolutely love, you can go ahead and purchase its usage rights and place directly onto your own t-shirts.

creativemarket.com – This is an online marketplace where you can browse and purchase all sorts of graphics, from web designs down to posters. It's excellent for a burst of creativity and inspiration.

Chapter 9 – Sell Your Own Photos

Instagram was created to be an image-sharing platform and, in spite of its many new features, its primary purpose remains unchanged: sharing photos with your friends across the globe. However, as a smart and cunning online entrepreneur you will recognize that photos are also *assets*. Photos can be branded, licensed and **sold** in many different ways and on a wide range of online marketplaces.

I have worked with many Instagram creators who are outstanding photographers and graphic designers; by selling their own photography and designs they have developed monthly incomes as high as $12,000.

Due to a tremendous lack in the skill, I have never used this approach myself. However, it can be a very straightforward high-earning opportunity if you are an excellent photographer or graphic designer. For this reason, I will still describe how YOU can make thousands of dollars each month selling Instagram photos or graphic designs in the following chapter.

Many artists sell direct copies of their Instagram posts, known as *Instagram prints*. For popular Instagram pages built on high-quality photography, I have seen prints easily sell in the range of $40-150. Other artists use Instagram to showcase some of their work and funnel followers to an online destination where they can purchase photography or designs directly.

How can you prevent people from stealing your photography?
If you showcase your photography on Instagram in high-resolution, people can visualize your photo and take a

screenshot to obtain a free copy. Of course, if you have licensed your photo you can sue them for theft and unauthorized use of your proprietary content. However, this is extremely expensive and time-consuming path.

The most common option is to showcase a low-resolution version of your photos on Instagram with a custom watermark filter that uniquely identifies the images as your property. If they wish to obtain a full-quality image without any form of branding they must purchase a copy from your website.

How to add custom watermark?

The following tools are extremely convenient to add custom watermarks/branding in your photos:

- **Adobe Photoshop**: most serious photographers have experience working with Adobe Photoshop. If you are a regular user, you will know just how easy it is to create and add a unique watermark to all your photos
- **WinWatermark.com** – this is a tool that was especially developed to easily create and implement unique watermarks. This tool comes in both free and paid-for versions.

www.Digimarc.com

This website offers unique image-tracking software that adds invisible watermarks to your photos; these allow you to identify any internet location where your image is displayed.

The main advantage of this platform is the invisible watermark. The main drawback is that it only points out where this image is being displayed without your authorization. Afterwards it is up to you to pursue a refund, which can be extremely difficult. Furthermore, not having a watermark often represents an incentive to steal your image instead of making a purchase. The yearly cost of this software is 50$, so you might wish to further research its features before purchasing.

Where can you sell your photos?

If you wish to sell your photos/designs online there are two main options for you to consider (1) online marketplace and (2) personal website.

Online Marketplace

There are many well-established online marketplaces where artists such as photographers and graphic designers can sell their work. These are websites where thousands of artists share their work, advertise it and offer it for purchase.

Advantages:
- Easy to set up your own profile and place photos for sale
- Marketplace already has customers

Disadvantages:
- You do not have full control of the style/portfolio/bio displayed
- You must pay a commission to the website
- Typically your work will find a lower price point on these marketplaces due to high competition

Recommended Options: These are the most popular marketplaces where artists can easily showcase and sell their photography/designs. I suggest visiting each of these websites

and explore their offers to fully evaluate how they can help you sell your work
- *500px.com*
- *Twenty20.com*

Your Personal Online Shop

Creating your online shop is a popular choice to sell photography and custom designs; most professional and high-earning artists follow this path. This choice is definitely more complex than a marketplace, but if done correctly a well-designed website can greatly boost your sales.

Advantages:
- You can control every aspect of the website: contact links, portfolio, BIO, etc...
- The professional look and lesser competition typically means your work will sell for a higher price range
- -You do not have to pay any commissions

Disadvantages:
- Website can be difficult and expensive to create
    - You can hire some excellent web developers at upwork.com
    - To create a website yourself, wordpress.com is the most popular choice
- You are responsible for 100% of your website visitors. You must have well-established following on Instagram or your website will not receive any traffic

Recommended Options:
- *Shopify.com* – as explained earlier this is the most popular online platform to create your own personal online store.

It contains well-established apps that allow customers to easily make purchases and pay directly into your bank account

- *Wordpress.com* – this is another very popular online platform that allows you to build your own website. This platform is free and is very well-known for its vast range of ready-made themes and templates available. You are not limited to creating an online store, but can build any type of website on this platform. If you are planning to build extensive portfolios and informational pages about yourself as a photographer/designer this may be a more appropriate choice.

Chapter 10 – Become Active on Multiple Social Media

Brands pay you depending on the total number of people you can influence, full stop.

On Instagram this is quantified using two parameters: total number of followers and audience engagement. If you wish to increase your Instagram income in a long-term fashion, your only choice is to increase one of the two above parameters.

A second option is to increase your reach as an influencer by diversifying your content distribution platforms beyond Instagram. Most influencers are active on multiple platforms to include Facebook, Twitter and Youtube; together these platforms report **billions** of monthly active users.

Becoming active on multiple platforms has a powerful synergistic effect, i.e. most of your Instagram are redirected to your YouTube account and your YouTube subscribers are redirected to your Instagram page.

It is critical you become active on multiple social media platforms to increase your total audience reach and thus receive significantly higher salaries in return.

It can be difficult to get started correctly on other social media platforms and YouTube if you only have Instagram experience. Each platform has its tricks and you must approach them correctly or you can severely damage your reputation.

You can check you some of my other Amazon guides to help you become active on multiple social media platforms and expand your reach as an influencer beyond Instagram.

Chapter 11 – The Importance of Photography

To this day, far too many still underestimate the importance of high *photo quality* in their accounts. Yes, the theme is important and yes hashtags are also important, but nothing quite compares to high-quality photos that capture and strike the viewer's attention. When your followers can't forget your photos – you, my friend, are a winner.

Although creating professional-grade images is beyond the scope of most Instagram profiles, learning the *technical basics of photography* can deliver tremendous improvements to most. If you are serious about Instagram, you must understand why a photo *'looks good'*.

In this book I will discuss the fundamentals of photography for the Instagram users. We will not study the history of photography or explore famous photographers and their unique styles or techniques. This book was designed with a very different goal**: create high-quality photos that make an impact on Instagram**.

Throughout this book we will focus on three main topics:

1. **Styles of Photography:** here we will explore the most popular and successful styles across Instagram. An infinity of square-on portrait photos or only landscape photos are boring, very boring – why not experiment with *macro* photography? Or a *bird's eye view* photo to keep things interesting?
2. **What to look for before pressing the shutter:** The outcome of your photos depends on an infinity of

factors. We will take a look at the most relevant ones, such as lighting, composition and focus.

3. **The importance of Editing:** Many amateur photographers choose to avoid editing altogether, but most professionals will tell you it is *essential*. We will discuss the fundamentals of editing, what apps you can use and some popular techniques that will make your photos creative and unique.

NOTE: THIS CHAPTER WAS TAKEN FROM MY MY NEW BOOK "**INSTAGRAM PHOTOGRAPHY**" - THE THIRD INSTALLMENT OF THE AMAZON BEST-SELLER SERIES "DOMINATING THE ISNTAGRAM GAME". *NOW AVAILABLE ON AMAZON.*

Conclusion

Thank you for reading this book, I hope you found it helpful!

I designed this guide to show readers how they can start making money from their Instagram accounts immediately. In today's Influencer marketing industry there are incredible opportunities and I want to help you take them.

In this guide I discussed the four most effective strategies you can use to earn money from Instagram. I chose these four because they represent the most popular, effective and lucrative opportunities today. These are:
- **Create Sponsored Content** (discussed in chapters 3-5)
- **Afilliate Marketing** (discussed in chapter 6)
- **Sell Your Own Product or Service** (discussed in chapter 7)
- **Selling Your Own Photos** (discussed in chapter 8)

Remember Rome was not built in a day! Do not get overwhelmed by Instagrammers who have millions of users. It takes time to establish a recognized social media presence and a loyal audience, please understand that!

Thank you for reading,

Pamela Russell

Made in the USA
Coppell, TX
07 July 2021